Poop Coloring Book

Something to Do While You Poo

If We Hold On

TOGETHER

The Six Shades of Poop

Brown: You're fine. Poop is naturally brown due to the bile produced in your liver

Black: It could mean that you're bleeding internally due to ulcer or cancer. Some vitamins containing iron or bismuth subsalicylate could cause black poop too. Pay attention if it's sticky, and see a doc if you're worried.

Green: Food may be movie through your large intestine too quicly. Or you could have eaten lots of green leafy veggies, or green food colouring.

Light-coloured, white, or clay-coloured: If it's not what you're normally seeing, it could mean a bile duct obstruction. Some medscould cause this too. See a doc.

Yellow: Greasy, foul-smelling yellow poop indicates excess fat, which could be due to a malabsorption disorder like celiac disease.

Blood-stained or Red: Blood in your poop could be a symptom of cancer. Always see a doc right away if you find blood in your stool.

All good poops which exist are the fruits of originality.

It is better to have pooped than never to have pooped at all.

Happiness is found in pooping, not merely possessing.

Release the
Kraken

PUMP A CLUMP
OF DUMP FROM
MY RUMP

Smelly Pooper   Smarty Pooper   Grumpy Pooper

Party Pooper   Cutie Pooper

Get your **SHIT** together

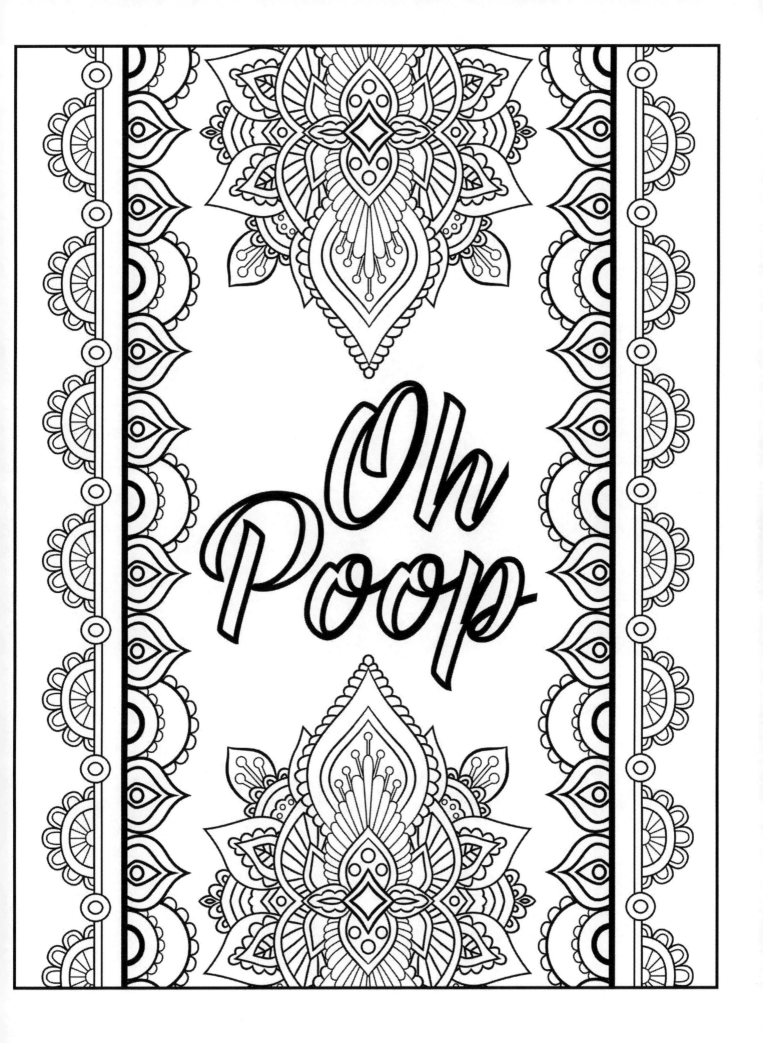

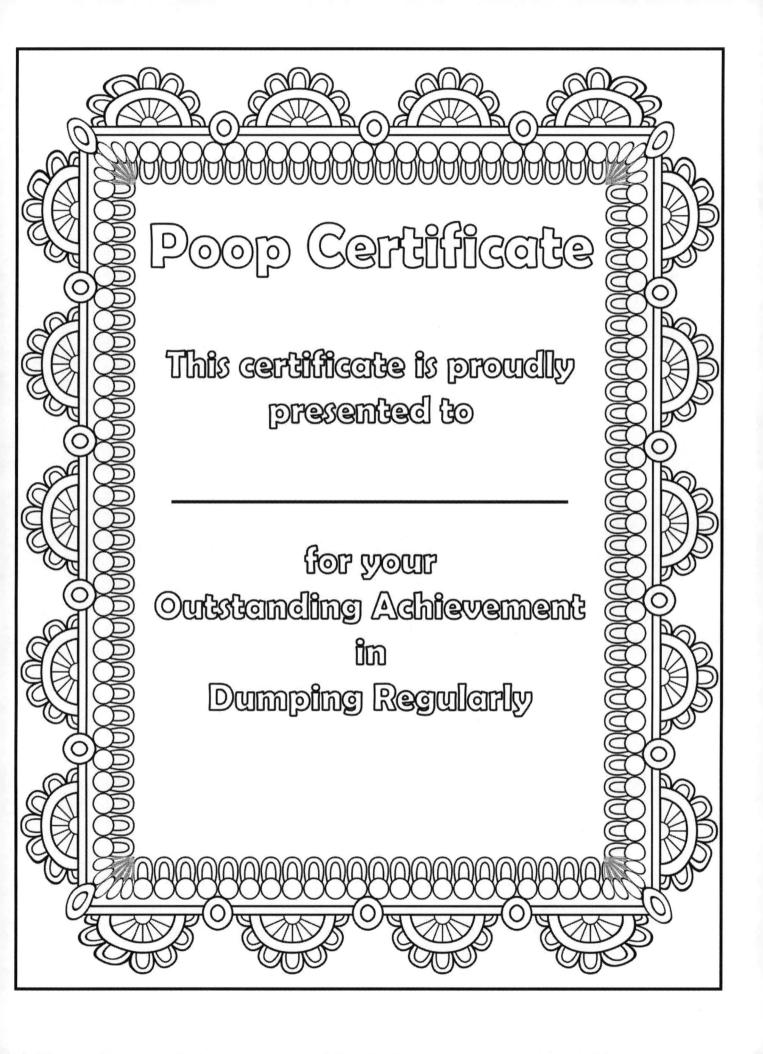

Poop Certificate

This certificate is proudly presented to

_____

for your
Outstanding Achievement
in
Dumping Regularly

Manufactured by Amazon.ca
Bolton, ON